"Good Morning, Mr. President"

"Good Morning, Mr. President"

A Story about Carl Sandburg

by Barbara Mitchell
illustrations by Dane Collins

A Carolrhoda Creative Minds Book

Carolrhoda Books, Inc./Minneapolis

For Shirley Lincoln Rigby and The Writers

Illustrations on pages 8, 10, 15, 17, and 26 by
George Overlie

Library of Congress Cataloging-in-Publication Data

Mitchell, Barbara, 1941-
    "Good morning, Mr. President" : a story about Carl Sandburg / by
Barbara Mitchell : illustrations by Dane Collins.
        p.   cm. — (A Carolrhoda creative minds book)
    Summary: Traces the life of the American poet, journalist, and
historian whose lifelong interest in Abraham Lincoln led to the
publishing of a multi-volume biography which won the Pulitzer Prize.
    ISBN 0-87614-329-X
    1. Sandburg, Carl, 1878-1967—Biography—Juvenile literature.
2. Lincoln, Abraham. 1809-1865—Juvenile literature. 3. Authors,
American—19th century—Biography—Juvenile literature.
[1. Sandburg, Carl. 1878-1967. 2. Poets, American.]   I. Collins,
Dane, ill.   II. Title.   III. Series.
PS3537.A618Z78 1988
811''.52—dc19
[B]
[92]   88-7265
                                                        CIP
                                                        AC

Manufactured in the United States of America

    3   4   5   6   7   8   9   10   98   97   96   95   94   93   92

Table of Contents

Chapter One

"Abraham Lincoln took a bath in that house," said the schoolboys whenever they passed by the mayor's house.

Mayor Henry R. Sanderson lived across the street from Churchill School, where Charlie Sandburg was in the eighth grade. "Think of it, Mart," Charlie said to his younger brother on a balmy spring day in 1891. "Lincoln took a bath right here in Galesburg."

The mayor of the little Illinois prairie town was out in front of his house, and Charlie wanted to stop and visit with him. Charlie loved history, and he loved people. He liked to hear people talk, to learn about what went on in their lives. But he had his job to see to.

Charlie Sandburg earned a silver dollar a week delivering the *Galesburg Republican-Register*. Every afternoon as soon as school was out, he folded 50 newspapers and set out to deliver them. Hurrying down Main Street, up Prairie, all the way over to Losey and back down Cherry, Charlie sent the news flying onto the doorsteps of Galesburg homes.

Each morning, Charlie delivered the newspapers from Chicago. The fat bundles arrived on the express train that roared into town at sunrise. Midway along his morning route, Charlie usually stopped at the grocery store to get warm. Around the glowing stove sat the old-timers of Galesburg. Charlie read the papers and listened to the men talk.

More often than not, the conversation was about Lincoln and "The War." The Civil War had been over for 26 years. It had been 33 years since Lincoln had come to Galesburg to debate Stephen A. Douglas on the issue of slavery. Lincoln and Douglas, in their race for the United States Senate, had made it a point to visit the fast-growing railroad town. The men who had sat listening to Lincoln tell his stories at supper that night in October 1858 never tired of retelling them.

"It's the truth," they said. "Lincoln could make a cat laugh."

Charlie liked a good story, too. As far back as he could remember, the Sandburgs had gathered around the kitchen table at night to listen to his mother's storytelling. Sometimes Clara Sandburg read from the big family Bible. Sometimes she told a Swedish folktale remembered from her girlhood. Often the story was about the 10 weeks she had spent on a ship crossing the Atlantic. Both Charlie's mother and father had come to America from Sweden.

After the storytelling, August Sandburg would take up his accordion and play a Swedish folk song. Charlie played along with his father on a banjo. Charlie had an ear for sound, August said.

Later, when the family was asleep, Charlie curled up in the chilly attic bedroom he shared with Mart and read far into the night. "I like good thick books," he told his brother.

As much as he loved learning, there was little chance of Charlie going to high school. Work was slow at the Chicago, Burlington & Quincy Railroad, where August Sandburg helped in the blacksmith's shop. The Sandburgs could afford to send only their eldest child, Mary, beyond grammar school. She was studying to be a teacher. Charlie left school after his eighth-grade graduation in December and went to work full-time.

The year 1892 was a hard one. In the fall, Charlie and his three younger brothers came down with diphtheria. Emil, age seven, and Freddie, age two, did not survive. His little sister, four-year-old Esther, miraculously escaped the disease. Charlie grieved for his little brothers and prayed that his mother, expecting a new baby, would stay well. By winter, work at the railroad was cut from 10 hours a day to 4, and Papa Sandburg's pay was cut in half. Early each morning, Charlie set off to work delivering milk.

Charlie always took a shortcut across the Knox College campus on his way to the dairy. There was something on the college grounds that intrigued him. On the east front of the Old Main Building was a bronze plate imprinted with words spoken by Lincoln and Douglas.

A crowd of twenty thousand people had gathered in Galesburg on the day of the Lincoln-Douglas Debate, October 7, 1858. The winds whipping across the prairie had been so strong that the red, white, and blue bunting on the speakers' stand was ripped nearly to shreds. The sturdy farmers and railroad workers had not minded the cold. Lincoln had had something to say, and they had wanted to hear it.

The cheering crowd was a part of history now. Charlie stood in the early morning stillness, reading from the bronze plate what Lincoln had said about slavery. He thought about the runaway slaves whom the people of Galesburg had hidden in the steeple of Old North Church. He thought about Lincoln.

Chapter Two

Each day, young Charlie Sandburg read the *Chicago Daily News* on his return trip to the dairy. The slow-moving milk wagon, its driver engrossed in the newspaper, was a familiar sight around Galesburg.

There was no time for reading on a bright afternoon in October 1896, though. Charlie had managed to deliver his milk in record time. Then he sent his horses at a fast clip in the direction of Knox College. The date was October 7. To celebrate the anniversary of the Lincoln-Douglas Debate, Lincoln's son, Robert Todd Lincoln, had been invited to speak.

Charlie wedged himself into the crowd in front of Old Main. The son of the Civil War president climbed to the speakers' stand. Charlie soon found himself thinking about Lincoln again. What had the president had to say to his son? he wondered. What would it be like to live in the White House?

What would it be like to leave Galesburg? Charlie asked himself. He was 18, now, and growing restless. Soon after Mary's graduation the following June, Charlie made a decision. Mary was independent. His wages were no longer necessary to pay for the clothes and books she had needed during teacher's training. The time had come for him to leave Galesburg. He broke the news to his parents at the end of the month. "I am going away," he said. "I am going to be a hobo."

There were many hobos during the 1890s, when work was scarce. These workers roved the country looking for jobs. Charlie wanted to work his way west and join the wheat harvesters.

August Sandburg scowled. Charlie had a job right in Galesburg. What need was there to go wandering about the country? Clara had tears in her eyes at noon dinner.

Charlie walked over to the railroad station after dinner. He didn't carry a suitcase. Everything he felt he would need—a pocketknife, needle and thread, his watch and razor, a cake of soap, and $3.25—was crammed into his pockets. A freight train, headed west, was just pulling out. Charlie hopped aboard. He stood in the doorway of a boxcar and watched the miles of corn fly by.

When the train clattered over the bridge that crossed the Mississippi River, Charlie shivered with excitement. He had left Illinois for the first time in his life. The train slowed down in Fort Madison, Iowa, and Charlie jumped off. He took a nickel of his money and celebrated by buying some cheese and crackers.

What would it be like to ride down the Mississippi, the great Father of Waters? Charlie wondered. He soon got a job loading kegs of nails onto a paddle wheeler. The rugged stevedores loading the steamboat had wonderful tales to tell. Charlie invested in two small notebooks and began to record the stories he was hearing and the words to the stevedores' songs.

Hopping freight trains again, Charlie worked his way west to Kansas City. There were always jobs to be found: waiting on tables, washing dishes, cutting weeds, working with railroad gangs. Wherever he went, there were tales to be told and songs to be sung. The other hobos shared both their food and their stories. Charlie's notebooks filled up with stories and songs of the American people and the "word pictures" he created. Charlie had begun to experiment with writing, trying to capture all that he saw.

19

Fall came, and Charlie headed back to Galesburg from Denver, where he had been washing dishes in a hotel. He had learned about himself, other people, and his country during his travels. But he was through with being a hobo for a while; he was happy to be going home.

Back in Galesburg, Charlie worked at odd jobs through the winter. In February 1898, he heard a rumor that President McKinley was considering going to war with Spain. The *Maine*, an American battleship, had been blown up in the port of Havana, Cuba. Across the country, there was excitement in the air. When the president declared war in April, Charlie was one of the first to join the Illinois Regiment.

The regiment was sent to Springfield, Illinois, for training. Springfield! That was where Abraham Lincoln had lived and worked as a lawyer for many years. It seemed that wherever he went, Charlie was met with some reminder of Lincoln. During his off-duty time, he visited Lincoln's home. When he returned to Galesburg on leave, he sported a dark blue uniform with brass buttons and pants made of light blue wool. "The same one the Union privates wore in Lincoln's war," he said proudly.

When the Illinois Regiment was sent to Falls Church, Virginia, Charlie took a trolley into Washington, D.C., so he could visit Ford's Theatre and Petersen House across the street. Standing in the dark of the theater where Lincoln had been shot and in the house where the assassinated president had died moved him deeply. Back in his bunk, he recited one of Lincoln's favorite poems to his soldier buddies. Lincoln was becoming a part of Charlie.

The Illinois Regiment was sent to Puerto Rico. While there, Charlie wrote letters to the *Galesburg Daily Mail.* When the newsmen from the hometown paper made him their official war correspondent, Charlie was thrilled. Once he had delivered newspapers—now he was writing for them!

Within five months, Charlie was back home. "Well," said his brother Mart, "you've been a hobo and you've been a soldier. What's next?"

"I think I'll go to college," Charlie said. As a veteran of the Spanish-American War, he was entitled to free tuition. He enrolled in Galesburg's Lombard College. Professor Philip Green Wright took a special interest in Charlie. Sandburg had a gift for writing, Wright said. He invited Charlie to join a select group of students known as the

Poor Writers' Club. "It isn't that we write poorly," Charlie assured his family and his friends with a grin. "It's just that none of us has ever sold anything."

To pay for his books, Charlie took a job as "call man" with the Prairie Street Firehouse. He was required to sleep at the firehouse at night and to report there during the daytime whenever the whistle blew. For this he was paid ten dollars a month. While the other firemen talked and played cards, Charlie lay in his bunk writing poetry. "You'll never make a real fireman," the other men teased. "Every time the whistle blows, you're caught up in that writing of yours."

Charlie would make a poet, though. Professor Wright was certain of it. In his basement print shop, Professor Wright printed 50 copies of a book of poems by Sandburg. Charlie proudly dedicated his first book to his mother.

The professor and "Cully" Sandburg, as Charlie was called by his college pals, had another interest in common. Professor Wright was fascinated with Lincoln. He and Charlie often spent entire evenings discussing the popular Civil War president. Professor Wright felt that people did not look beyond the well-loved stories of Lincoln's life.

It was impossible to see Lincoln as a real human being. Charlie agreed. "Someday, I am going to really study Lincoln and get to understand him," he vowed.

Chapter Three

Charlie left college suddenly in 1902. He had taken courses only in the areas that interested him: Latin, English, chemistry, drama, and public speaking. "What's the use of cluttering up my brain with things I will not use?" he had asked.

"Well, what are you going to do now?" Mart asked.

The truth was, Charlie did not know what he wanted to do.

"But I can tell you one thing for sure," he said.

"No matter what else happens, I'll do a lot of fooling around with pens and pencils and paper."

"Is there any money in this writing business, Charlie?" his father wanted to know.

"I guess, Papa, all I have is hope," Charlie replied. Two editors had already returned the envelope of poems he had sent out. Was there enough money in writing to earn a living? Charlie was not sure. What he did know was that he *had* to be a writer.

For the next few years, Charlie traveled on trains, this time crisscrossing the eastern part of the United States. He worked at odd jobs and wrote about everything he saw and felt. In 1905, he went to Chicago where he wrote for several different small magazines and sometimes did editorial work, as well.

On his time off, Charlie roamed the city or rode his bike in the country. He stopped to look at factories and to talk to policemen on street corners. He sat beside lonely country roads. All that he heard and saw went into his "word pictures." Poetry was the form of writing he liked working on best, although it brought him no money.

Charlie was writing for the *Daily Socialist* when his fiery writing on behalf of the working class caught the attention of the organizer for the Social-Democratic Party in Wisconsin. "How would you like to become a party organizer?" the Wisconsin organizer asked.

Charlie's anger over the wrongs done to the workers and the poor people of America was strong. He joined the party and accepted the job. One day in 1907, while visiting the office of the Wisconsin Social-Democratic Party leader in Milwaukee, Charlie met an attractive young woman named Lilian Steichen. Lilian was an enthusiastic socialist, too. Charlie found himself asking Lilian if he might accompany her on her walk to the streetcar at the end of the day.

Lilian also loved to read. "And I write poetry," she confessed. "I call my poems word melodies." She and Charlie found their interest in one another growing fast.

The Steichens had a pet name for their daughter. They called her Paus'l. Charlie called her Paula.

"Why don't you use the Swedish form of your first name?" Paula asked Charlie. She much preferred the name *Carl* to *Charlie*. She thought it sounded more masculine.

All the boys in grammar school had Americanized their names, Charlie explained. Although he had been christened Carl, everyone had called him Charlie from second grade on. "But I would be willing to become Carl again for you," he said. So Charlie became Carl Sandburg.

The following June, Paula and Carl were married. They moved to a tiny apartment in Appleton, Wisconsin, where Carl was working for the Social-Democratic Party. The young couple needed money, though, and soon they moved to Milwaukee, where Carl took a job writing advertising copy for a department store. His well-written ads caught the attention of the local newspaper editors. Carl was hired by the *Milwaukee Journal*. He quickly moved on to the *Milwaukee Daily News* as an editorial writer.

Carl came home from work one snowy February night with exciting news. In honor of the 100th anniversary of the birth of Abraham Lincoln, the United States government was going to put Lincoln's face on the new 1909 penny. "Lincoln on the common folks' coin!" Carl exclaimed. "It's a stroke of genius!" He sat down and wrote an editorial praising the government for its good judgment.

Paula was happy to see her husband's enthusiasm. Carl had been discouraged lately. He had been sending his poems out to magazines, hoping to have them published. But the envelopes full of poems came back almost as soon as they were mailed. Carl was taking the rejections hard.

In 1911, the Sandburgs' first child, Margaret, was born. The following year, a pressmen's strike in Chicago shut down the major newspapers there. The *Chicago Daily Socialist* became the city's only newspaper. Taking advantage of this opportunity, the paper changed its name to the *Chicago Daily World*. Its circulation soared to six hundred thousand readers a day. The paper needed reporters, and Carl had always wanted to write for a major Chicago newspaper. The Sandburgs moved to Chicago, and his dream was realized.

When the strike was ended, business at the *World* plummeted. Carl was fired. The postman continued to bring rejection slips from poetry publishers. *Could* a man support a family by being a writer? Carl began to doubt it. After months of no steady work, he was finally hired by an experimental new newspaper known as the *Day Book*.

Paula kept sending out Carl's poems. It was shortly after their second daughter, Janet, was born, in the winter of 1914, that Paula discovered a two-year-old magazine called *Poetry: A Magazine of Verse*.

The editor, a woman named Harriet Monroe, was known to be bold and willing to take the risk of introducing new poets. Paula selected nine of what she felt were Carl's very best poems and mailed them off to the magazine. The packet included "In a Back Alley," one of Carl's own favorites. It was about Abraham Lincoln.

The rest of the poems were about Chicago. The smoky industrial city fascinated Carl Sandburg. Paula said her husband and Chicago were made for each other. The poems Carl was writing were sturdy and strong. "They are the voice of the American people," Paula told him. "We simply must get them published."

Secretly, Paula worried. Carl's poems didn't rhyme. "Why should I use a word that isn't the right word simply because it rhymes?" he asked. Carl didn't worry about keeping a steady rhythm either. When he got excited, the words bounced ahead. When he was deeply moved, they slowed down. "A poet cries his heart out in the best way he can," he said.

People in the literary world in 1914 expected poetry to have elegance. They expected it to follow the rules. Would an editor see Carl's writing as poetry? Paula wasn't sure.

When Harriet Monroe opened the little packet of poems, she took a deep breath and swallowed. This writing was shocking:

CHICAGO

Hog Butcher for the World,
Tool Maker, Stacker of Wheat,
Player with Railroads and the Nation's Freight Handler;
Stormy, husky, brawling,
City of the Big Shoulders:

.   .   .   .

Harriet Monroe carried the startling poems to her assistant. "What kind of poet writes about hog butchering?" she asked. "And listen to this:"

IN A BACK ALLEY

Remembrance for a great man is this.
The newsies are pitching pennies.
And on the copper disk is the man's face.
Dead lover of boys, what do you ask for now?

"*Newsies*. What kind of word is that?" the assistant, Alice Corbin, asked.

"It's slang, that's what," Ms. Monroe replied. "And what kind of poet writes about back alleys?"

Ms. Corbin was quiet for a moment. "Read those last two lines again," she said softly.

Harriet read the lines. Her assistant was moved— that she could see. This was poetry, all right. But could she afford to risk the reputation of her new magazine on it?

She went back to her office deep in thought.

Chapter Four

The March 1914 issue of *Poetry* was the boldest yet. The first page introduced a set of poems by a daring new American poet—Carl Sandburg.

"Jargon!" "Nonpoetry!" the literary critics cried. But Harriet Monroe and Alice Corbin were not dismayed. They had made a discovery, and they knew it. On her next trip to New York, Alice Corbin carried a packet of Sandburg's poems with her to show Alfred Harcourt, a book salesman with Henry Holt & Company. Harcourt had read the Sandburg poems published in *Poetry* and had contacted Alice Corbin during a visit to Chicago. He wanted to see more of Sandburg's poems.

Alice Corbin showed Alfred Harcourt the poems Carl had been working on for several years. There were 260 of them all together. The 100 selected by the editors at Henry Holt & Company became *Chicago Poems*, Sandburg's first professionally published book. At the age of 38, Carl Sandburg had secured a place for himself in the literary world.

The publication of *Chicago Poems* caused a stir. Chicago news writers, editors, and publishers were especially interested in the poems of one of their own.

"There's a fine writer you ought to have," newspaperman Ben Hecht told the *Chicago Daily News*'s news editor, Henry Justin Smith.

"The *News* is overstaffed," Smith said brusquely.

"He writes superb poetry," Hecht added.

Smith looked up from his desk. "What kind of poetry?"

Smith had a soft spot for poetry, and Hecht knew it. "The new kind!" he said. "Good stuff."

"Send him over," Smith said. Carl was hired.

Life at Chicago's busiest newspaper was hectic. Carl covered labor stories and wrote features and editorials. His boss noticed that the new employee was forever scribbling poetry on scraps of paper, but Smith didn't mind. In fact, he encouraged Carl's poetry writing; the fellow had talent, Smith thought.

In 1919, Carl began filling in for the *News's* motion picture editor. When the editor quit, Carl assumed his position. This new work gave him more time for his poetry. Carl saw half a dozen movies each weekend. On Mondays and Tuesdays, he wrote his reviews. The rest of the week he had free for writing poetry. Within two years after the publication of *Chicago Poems* he had turned out *Cornhuskers*, another large book of poems. In *Cornhuskers*, he moved from the big city to the prairies and little towns that dotted the Midwest. The new book contained a poem on Lincoln, of course. "Knucks" recalled Carl's impressions of Abraham Lincoln's town, stored in the poet's memory since his Springfield army days.

The year 1918 brought the birth of Helga, the Sandburg's third daughter. The year 1920 brought the birth of yet another book of poetry, entitled *Smoke and Steel*. It also brought Carl's first invitation to do a reading of his poems. Carl

Sandburg was recognized as a respected poet now. He was asked to go to Cornell College in Mount Vernon, Iowa, and read to the students.

Carl wrote a special new poem for the occasion, a Lincoln poem. On the night of the performance, he strode casually onstage, perched himself on a high stool, and began to read about Abraham Lincoln's mother:

FIRE-LOGS

Nancy Hanks dreams by the fire;
Dreams, and the logs sputter,
And the yellow tongues climb.
Red lines lick their way in flickers.
Oh, sputter, logs.
      Oh, dream, Nancy.
Time now for a beautiful child.
Time now for a tall man to come.

Carl had a magical way with his voice. The fire logs sputtered. The yellow flames flickered. His voice became soft, dreamy. The students were transported back to the plain little cabin where Lincoln was born.

For a full hour, Carl sat up on the stage reading his poems and giving his reflections on life in America.

"And now I will sing a few folk songs that somehow tie into the folk quality I've tried to get into my verse," he said. "If you don't care for them and want to leave the hall, it will be all right with me. I'd only be doing what I'd be doing at home anyway." With that, he disappeared behind the speakers' stand.

He emerged with a guitar in hand and soon filled the room with songs of the American people. During his wanderings about the country, he had collected nearly three hundred songs and was working them into a book that would be called *American Songbag*. There was a Lincoln song, of course. "Old Abe Lincoln Came Out of the Wilderness" had been sung by torchlight processions of Republicans in the summer of 1860, Carl told his listeners. Tad and Willie Lincoln had sung it to their father. Carl sang for another hour. Not a student left the hall.

Requests for readings began to come in from all over the country. Before accepting an engagement, Carl had a pair of stock questions. "Is there anyone in town who knew Lincoln? Does the library have a Lincoln collection?" If the possibility existed for adding to his growing collection of Lincoln lore, he accepted an invitation immediately. If not, he was likely to turn the offer down.

In 1923, Alfred Harcourt invited Carl to lunch with him in New York. He had a book idea he wished to discuss. "What would you think of turning your interest in Lincoln into a book for teenage readers?" Harcourt asked.

"I have been thinking of that very thing for quite some time now," Carl confessed.

Carl had already published two successful books for children. His *Rootabaga Stories* and *Rootabaga Pigeons* had grown out of the stories he made up for Margaret, Janet, and Helga. Now he threw himself into research for the Lincoln book. His first task was to sort out the materials he had been collecting for years. "Rather like sorting oranges," he said.

Next, Carl began to explore firsthand the places the Lincoln family had lived, beginning with the Lincoln family homestead in Virginia. The more he learned about Lincoln, the more he realized the Civil War president had had interests much like his own. Lincoln had loved to talk and listen to talk. He had worked on the Mississippi and had read "good thick books" all his life.

Lincoln, Carl found, could be as strong as steel

and as soft as velvet. Lincoln laughed, and Lincoln cried. Lincoln got angry. Lincoln failed. It was just as Carl had always thought. Abraham Lincoln was far more than a fairy-tale hero. Lincoln was human.

Carl decided that *Abraham Lincoln: The Prairie Years* would cover Lincoln's life from his Virginia ancestors up until the time he became president. The story took two years to write. Carl delivered the manuscript to Harcourt early in 1925. He had succeeded more than any other author in taking the sentimentality out of Lincoln's story. There was one problem, though—the manuscript was 900 pages long.

"A bit much for young readers, don't you think?" Harcourt commented. The book was long, yes, but the editor could see it was a gem. The decision was made to publish it for the adult market. The remarkable two-volume story sold 48,000 copies its first year. A teenage edition, covering the first 26 chapters, was published two years later.

With the publication of his Lincoln story, Carl Sandburg felt financially secure for the first time in his life. Yes, there was money to be made in the writing business. Carl and Paula turned their summer home on the dunes high above Lake

Michigan into a permanent living place. Carl was able to leave the newspaper business, although he continued to write an editorial column. He needed time and a peaceful place to write. At age 50, he had an exciting new project in mind.

Chapter Five

Carl's new project again had to do with Lincoln. What he had in mind was an epilogue to *The Prairie Years*. "Nothing too involved," he explained to his editor, "just a little follow-up." He felt it would give readers a glimpse of Lincoln as president and entice them to go back and read the first two-volume book.

No sooner did the Sandburgs settle into their shore home, than the attic began to fill up with Lincoln lore.

Carl installed a stove, a cot, and some comfortable chairs in the attic. He placed his typewriter on top of a wooden crate and sat down to write the three-chapter story.

As always, Carl threw himself into the project at hand. He set up a schedule. Mornings he would spend with Paula—visiting her herd of prizewinning goats and often chatting with the neighbors. Afternoons would be given to answering letters and writing his newspaper column. Evenings would be for the family, with song and storytelling sessions around the fireplace. Hardly a day went by that Carl did not pick up his guitar. At night, when the house was still, he would work on his little Lincoln story.

Often Carl wrote into the wee hours of the morning. Sometimes Paula or one of the girls would silently place a steaming pot of coffee and a breakfast tray at the door, then tiptoe away. It was not long before the epilogue developed into a substantial piece of work. Carl pored over more than a thousand books on Lincoln, marking the pages he wished to have copied and passing them on to Paula.

The writer's young daughters were often called upon to sort materials. "Do we *have* to classify?"

the girls would ask on beautiful beach days. But both they and their father recalled the "classifying days" with fondness long after the book was written.

In time, it became necessary to hire two secretaries. The second floor was piled high with newspapers, posters, and pamphlets, all about Lincoln. The mushrooming collection spilled over into the barn. Carl worked amidst a clutter of boxes full of large envelopes, each one stuffed with information on a different facet of Lincoln. What had begun as a three-chapter story had developed into *Abraham Lincoln: The War Years*, a full-fledged book. Lincoln had taken hold of Carl Sandburg once again.

The Sandburgs' neighbors were well aware of his new book project. Carl was never secretive about his work. Every morning during the hour after sunrise, the author walked along the edge of Lake Michigan, pondering what he would add to his story. You could set your watch by him, the neighbors said.

Carl's punctuality inspired his neighbors to play a joke on him. They hired a tall, lean actor and dressed him up in a long coat and stovepipe hat. When it was time for Carl's walk, they stationed the actor at the other end of the beach.

"Meet Sandburg midway along the beach," they instructed him. The neighbors climbed to the top of a dune to watch the fun.

Along came Carl, head down, hands beating time to the rhythm of the words he planned to add to his book that night. The top-hatted actor began his walk. The two figures moved closer and closer together. At the middle of the beach, they met. Carl looked up, just for a moment, then he moved on, head bent toward the sand, just as before.

When the costumed actor rejoined the neighbors, he was breathless and his face was as white as the sand.

"What did he do?" asked the jokers. "What did he say?"

"He bowed," he replied.

"Well, didn't he *say* anything?" the neighbors demanded.

"It was just after he bowed," explained the shaken actor. "He said...he said, 'Good morning, Mr. President.'"

Eleven years after Carl began writing his Lincoln epilogue, the final page rested in the typewriter. The Sandburgs' housekeeper read this last page when she was dusting the attic workroom. Carl

Sandburg's poetic writing style moved the housekeeper. "I read the closing words and burst into tears," she confessed to Helga.

The housckeeper was not the only member of the household who cried that day in 1939. During the years Carl spent thinking and writing about Lincoln, the long-dead president was his constant companion. The realization that they would be parting after so much time hit Carl hard.

Carl went to his typewriter and rolled out the final page. His eyes began to sting. For an hour, two hours, and more, the tears ran down his cheeks. Carl Sandburg was not ashamed.

The completed manuscript was 3,400 pages long—1,200,000 words. The story was longer than the Bible, longer than the complete works of Shakespeare.

Abraham Lincoln: The War Years was published in four volumes in December 1939. Reporters covering the story of the publication were astounded at the amount of work Carl had done.

"How in the world did you do it?" they asked.

Carl grinned. "That son-of-a-gun Lincoln grows on you," he said.

AFTERWORD

In 1940, Carl Sandburg was awarded the Pulitzer Prize for his great contribution to American history. A complete collection of his poems—over eight hundred of them—won him a second Pulitzer in 1950.

In 1945, a Galesburg teacher, Mrs. Adda Gentry George, began working for the restoration of the Carl Sandburg birthplace. The little house at 333 Third Street was dedicated on October 7, 1946, the 88th anniversary of the Lincoln-Douglas

Debate. Carl was immensely pleased but did not attend. It would be immodest, he said. When he later went to see the restored home for himself, a reporter asked, "Did you actually sleep in that bed?"

Carl lay down on the bed. He closed his eyes briefly, then got up. "Now you can say that I did," he said.

Schoolchildren from all over America help maintain the birthplace. In 1961, the children of Galesburg honored their poet on his birthday with a penny parade. Bags, boxes, and pillowcases stuffed with 43,360 pennies were toted to the bank, accompanied by a police escort. January 6 has been a fun-filled Penny Day in Galesburg ever since.

President Lyndon B. Johnson honored Carl Sandburg in 1964 with the Freedom Medal for his contribution to the American people's understanding of their land and its history. Sandburg's last book, *Honey and Salt*, was published on his 88th birthday. The much-loved American author continued to write every day of his life. He died at the age of 89 at Connemara, the Sandburgs' retirement home in Flat Rock, North Carolina, on July 22, 1967.

BOOKLIST

Carl Sandburg had a special feeling for children. His writings for young people include collections of poetry, stories, an autobiography, and, of course, a book about Abraham Lincoln. Listed below are some of Carl Sandburg's books for young readers.

* ***Abe Lincoln Grows Up*** Harcourt Brace Jovanovich. Illustrated by James Daugherty. *Biography*

  The American Songbag Harcourt Brace Jovanovich. *Songs*

* ***Early Moon*** Harcourt Brace Jovanovich. Illustrated by James Daugherty. *Poetry*

* ***Prairie-Town Boy*** Harcourt Brace Jovanovich. Illustrated by Joe Krush. *Autobiography*

* ***Rootabaga Stories*** Harcourt Brace Jovanovich. Illustrations and decorations by Maude and Miska Petersham. (Contains *Rootabaga Stories and Rootabaga Pigeons.*) *Stories*

(continued on next page)

Rainbows Are Made: Poems by Carl Sandburg, selected by Lee Bennett Hopkins. Harcourt Brace Jovanovich. With wood engravings by Fritz Eichenberg. *Poetry*

* ***Wind Song*** Harcourt Brace Jovanovich. Illustrated by William A. Smith. *Poetry*

* These books are also included in ***The Sandburg Treasury: Prose and Poetry for Young People***, Introduction by Paula Sandburg. Harcourt Brace Jovanovich. Illustrated by Paul Bacon.

Acknowledgments

"Chicago" and "In a Back Alley" from CHICAGO POEMS by Carl Sandburg, copyright 1916 by Holt, Rinehart and Winston, Inc.; renewed 1944 by Carl Sandburg. Reprinted by permission of Harcourt Brace Jovanovich, Inc.

"Fire-Logs" from CORNHUSKERS by Carl Sandburg, copyright 1918 by Holt, Rinehart and Winston, Inc.; renewed 1946 by Carl Sandburg. Reprinted by permission of Harcourt Brace Jovanovich, Inc.